Taking Time for Marriage

E. Ray Jerkins

BAKER BOOK HOUSE
Grand Rapids, Michigan 49506

Copyright 1977 by
Gospel Advocate Company
Trade edition issued 1982 by
Baker Book House Company
with permission of copyright owner

ISBN: 0-8010-5189-4

Printed in the United States of America

To my wife,
Geraldine,
who has been my source of inspiration
over the years, a wonderful partner

Contents

Preface   7

1. Taking Time for Marriage   11

2. Time for "T"   15

3. Time for "I"   31

4. Time for "M"   41

5. Time for "E"   51

Preface

As a marriage and family counselor, I realize that I work in many very delicate situations. I am constantly aware of the fact that the decisions and suggestions that I offer will affect many lives. The magnitude of this responsibility is further emphasized when I continually remind myself that I will have to give an answer to the Creator.

The family is the oldest divine institution of which we know. However, many people seem to have forgotten the purpose that God had for the involvement of man and woman, male and female. After God had created Adam, He placed him in the Garden of Eden and he was alone. There was nothing with him—no animals, birds, or other human beings. "And the LORD God said, It is not good that the man should be alone; I will make him an help meet for him" (Gen. 2:18). Thus the family was established so that Adam and Eve could be companions for each other.

In the family, we should never feel that we are alone. However, in our society, this seems to be an area in which we have failed. Husbands are so busy earning a living and so many wives are working outside the home that they fail to spend time together to develop the wonderful relationship of husband and wife. It takes time to grow a garden and to get an education, and it takes time to build a strong, happy marriage.

I am convinced that we need to restudy Ephesians 5:22–33, where Paul talks about the husband-wife relationship. If you listed the responsibilities of the husband and the wife as he outlines them, you would have this:

Husband's Responsibilities	Wife's Responsibilities
love your wife as Christ loved the church (v. 25)	submit to your husband (v. 22)
love your wife as you love your own body (v. 28)	be subject to your husband (v. 24)
love your wife even as yourself (v. 33)	revere your husband (v. 33)
protect your wife (v. 23)	
nourish and cherish your wife (v. 29)	

We have long heard that if we want to have better homes, we should change the women. I am convinced that if we want better homes we need to improve the husbands. We need husbands who love their wives in the way Paul describes in Ephesians. We need husbands who are willing to give of themselves to their families. We need husbands who realize that earning a living is only a part of their responsibilities and that their work is never done because they have family activity after their day's work is over. We need husbands who will lead their families with love and consideration, displaying kindness and great spiritual values. When we reach this level of leadership in the home, you will see a change in our nation and in the church.

I do not mean to leave the impression that husbands have to do all of the changing, giving, doing, and sacrificing. Wives have their duties also. But it will be easier to ". . . love their husbands, to love their children, . . . [be] keepers at home, good, obedient to their own husbands . . ." (Titus 2:4–5) when wives realize their husbands are sharing themselves and displaying a love for them that is equal to the husbands' love for themselves.

I have not discussed all of the important things in marriage that can make your home more enjoyable. It is my hope that the things presented will encourage you to think about things that you can do to have a happy home.

1
Taking Time for Marriage

We are living in a time that is unusual. The greatest dangers the family has ever known are present now. At no other time has the divorce rate been as high as it is currently. In 1981 there were 2.3 million marriages, and there were 1.2 million divorces!

It is difficult for us to understand what is happening to the family, and as a result of this, more and more books are being written to help the family survive. I believe the greatest asset we have in keeping the family alive and helping it to succeed is *time*.

Our Bill of Rights declares that all men are created equal. We have political equality, yes, but equality in other areas, no. We all realize that this is true. However, there is only one area in which I know there is absolute equality and that is the amount of time per day that each of us has. Regardless of where you live in the United States, or in the world, there are sixty seconds to every minute and sixty minutes to every hour and 24 hours to every day. This means that every person, whether he is highly educated or never had the opportunity for education, exceedingly wealthy or living in poverty, has 168 hours every week or 8,760 hours per year. The rich man does not have more hours than the poor, or the poor more hours than the rich. Each of us has the same amount of time.

The Bible emphasizes the fact that time is important. One of the outstanding passages of the Bible is Ecclesiastes 3:1–8. The writer says, "To every thing there is a season, and a time to every purpose under the heaven: a time to be born, and a time to die; a time to plant, and a time to pluck up that which is planted; a time to kill, and a time to heal; a time to break down, and a time to build up; a time to weep, and a time to laugh; a time to mourn, and a time to dance; a time to cast away stones, and a time to gather stones together; a time to embrace, and a time to refrain from embracing; a time to get, and a time to lose; a time to keep, and a time to cast away; a time to rend, and a time to sew; a time to keep silence and a time to speak; a time to love, and a time to hate; a time of war, and a time of peace." The writer emphasizes that life is made of time. What we do with our time determines what we do with our lives. To put it another way, what we do with our lives determines how well we use our time.

In this nuclear age in which the family is trying to survive, more and more pressures are being placed upon it. The great corporations are placing obstacles in the way of family unity and family happiness. They are demanding more travel and more frequent change of residence. Seemingly they plan those things that appeal to the unattached individual rather than the family. Because of travel, husbands and wives many times live in isolation from each other and children are constantly abandoned by fathers and mothers who fight for success in business. Such children are oftentimes as emotionally abandoned as the children in the ghetto. These families' lives never mesh. There is enough money but these parents are using their time primarily to make money and not dividing their time correctly between things and family. There is enough money, but there is too much emotional distance in the family.

It is my purpose to help you use your time wisely and effectively. For that reason I present a simple series of thoughts based on the idea of time, for it is my personal conviction that the proper use of time will improve family life. I am presenting the thought of time in such a way that it will be easily remembered and related to. Remember, if things go well with the family, life is worth living; but when the family falters, life falls apart. Then where do you go?

Many times marriage is pictured as a form of boredom, imprisonment, or oppression, but this is not so. Marriage is an assault on loneliness and it is a threat to the solitary individual. Marriage does impose frustrating responsibilities yet tremendously rewarding pleasures. So marriage is not for the immature but for the mature, and children soon become welcome responsibilities, pointing out that we are no longer children but mature adults who pass on to future generations a part of us.

In marriage, remember that you have many different roles. The family is made up of the husband and wife and children, but each of these assumes different responsibilities. You are not just a husband but you are also a father, a son, possibly a brother, or an uncle, or a cousin. You are not just a wife, but you are a daughter, possibly a sister, an aunt, or a cousin. You are not merely a child, but you are a grandson or a granddaughter, or a brother, or a sister, or an aunt or uncle. So you see this becomes a family network. How we do in this family network depends on how well we use our time. How well we use our time depends on how well we know how to use our time.

I will organize the following chapters on the basis of using the word *time* as an acrostic, in which "T" will stand for particular traits that are necessary in the family; "I" will stand for others; "M" and "E" will stand for still other qualities.

Taking time for marriage is the key to having a good marriage. Using time wisely is necessary to have a good marriage.

2
Time For "T"

I will certainly not exhaust all the subjects that I might put in this area, but I think some are outstanding. Neither will these thoughts be presented in order of importance. However, let me begin this aspect of taking time for marriage with what I believe is probably an outstanding necessity for a good marriage.

Talk

In our society it is tragic when we see someone who is unable to talk. The word that describes this has taken on many other meanings, and that word is "dumb." If a person is unable to speak we say he is dumb. Therefore, we talk about deaf, blind, and mute, or deaf, blind, and dumb. A person who cannot speak because of a genetic speech defect would not necessarily be considered dumb but this word is applied to one who is unable to speak because we do not know of his intelligence, ideas, intentions, purposes, aims, or goals. Because he cannot express himself, history has given the meaning of the word *dumb* to one who cannot speak.

I am not saying a married person who does not talk is dumb, but I am saying that talking to your mate is important. Talking is communication. There are many people who say, "I just don't talk. I don't like to talk."

Many of my remarks will be directed primarily to husbands. I do not know why unwillingness to talk affects men more than women. This was impressed on me not long ago when I was doing some research in my counseling files. I have all my clients write out a list of things that their spouses do that upset them and what they do that upsets their spouses. In the hundreds of cases I have worked with I have found that when the wife makes a list of what her husband does that upsets her, invariably I will find the statement, "He does not talk to me." And in the same situation, when the husband makes a list of what he does that upsets his wife, it will usually include, "I do not talk to her." In fewer than one-half of 1 percent of the cases will I have the wives making the statement they don't talk to their husbands or the husbands saying, "My wife will not talk to me." For this reason I find that reluctance to talk seems to be a problem that men have—a problem of communicating with their wives, a problem of sharing themselves with their wives.

What do you talk about at your house? When the husband leaves home every morning and goes to work, it puts him in contact with people, things, and happenings. He can relate to these. He can either like the people or not like them, joke with them, talk with them, or be with them. But in the household activity in which many wives find themselves, they have conversation with the children, and their housework. Often this does not demand a great deal of thinking upon their part. When the husband—another adult with whom the wife can relate—comes home in the evening, she is interested in talking with him. His general thinking is, "I have been talking all day, so why do I have to talk now that I am home?" But at this time she is interested in adult conversation. All day there has been juvenile conversation and now she is interested in talking with him.

To carry on a conversation one must ask questions, so the wife asks a question about her husband's work or about the people he saw, or about anything exciting that might have happened, and in response she gets only a grunt. Then he believes that she is nagging him and as a result of this he becomes irritated. All she is trying to do is to have an emotional or intellectual relationship with her husband.

One of the greatest things a husband can do to make a marriage really enjoyable is to talk to his wife. Someone says, "What can I talk about?" Your conversation does not have to be one of depth, dealing with the philosophical or political backgrounds of the world. Your conversation can be merely chit-chat. For instance, you can talk to your wife about television programs you are watching together, political situations of our day, the blooming of the trees or the growing of the grass, the birds that are in the yard, some hobbies that both of you might have, the children and their activities, your past life, your families, or whatever happens to be said on the radio at that time. There are a lot of things you can talk about. You may think that it is not necessary to talk. I believe it is important.

A woman once sat down in my office and said, "Mr. Jerkins, my husband will not talk to me." On further investigation, I found that he did talk to her only if necessary and only about things that were of absolute importance. There was no small talk. Later, the husband said his wife's comment was true. He spoke only if spoken to. He talked to his wife only if he was asking for a particular thing. When the children asked him a question he answered, but there was no sharing of his mind through conversation with his wife or children. As a result his family assumed several things. First, they assumed that he was not interested in sharing himself with them. Second, they therefore assumed that they were not important enough to be a part of his life. Third, they assumed that he did not like them. Fourth, they assumed that he thought they were so ignorant that they could not converse with him. When I said this, the man replied, "These are not my thoughts; I just do not talk." He needs to learn that sharing himself through conversation is the way that God intended us to be. We need to take time for talking. You need to set aside a time every day for this. Be sure that you talk to your spouse every day. Instead of sitting at the table and watching television during the meal or reading the paper, let this be a pleasant time for conversation. Husbands, when you come in from work, show an interest in your wife—what she did that day, how things are at the house, what is happening with things of nature or the children—almost anything, but at least let her know that you are interested in her by talking to her.

There is no greater way of sharing your mind, emotions, feelings, ideas, goals, and aspirations than by talking. Take time to talk.

Tasks

In marriage and family life there are certain responsibilities that we have to face. Many of us would like to remain children all of our lives and have somebody else make the decisions for us and do the things that are unpleasant for us. However, when we marry we are telling the world that we are no longer children but accept the responsibilities of a spouse, a home, a family, taking care of our home, our yard, our car, and other physical things. There are things around the house that are not the most enjoyable things to do.

You must take time for tasks. Let me illustrate. In one case I found that one of the major difficulties was that neither the husband nor the wife was taking time for the tasks around the house. For more than two years the mailbox had not been put up. Curtains had not been placed in the house because the wife had never gotten around to it. Things were still in boxes because she kept getting things from the boxes rather than putting them in the cabinets for which they had ample space. Putting the cabinets up was just too much trouble. Flowers had not been planted outside because it was too much trouble for the husband to prepare the bed for flowers or to have shrubbery set out to enhance the beauty of the house. The windows had not been washed on the inside for several years because the wife did not want to do it. The husband had not washed the outside because she had not cleaned the inside first. So the stickers that are placed on new windows were still there even after this couple had been living in this house for more than two years. And the list could go on and on.

It is easy to see in a situation like this that the couple had tasks that needed to be done but did not want to do them. Evidently they thought that if they did not do these chores that somebody would come along and put up the mailbox, or wash their windows, or plant their trees. When you marry you accept the fact that there are responsibilities around the house.

After a period of time the house will need paint, the yard will need work, the driveway will need repair, the windows will need to be washed, and the house will need to be cleaned. These are not delightful tasks but they have to be done. I recommend that you take time to do them.

How do you take time for tasks that are unpleasant? The best way is to make a list of those things that need to be done and then estimate how long you think it will take you to do them. By taking each task separately, you can accomplish things little by little. For instance, in the case just mentioned, putting up a mailbox amounted to less than thirty minutes. Washing the windows would amount to less than half a day. As you make your list of things that need to be done, note the time necessary to do them. Then rearrange your list to indicate which task needs to be done first. Start with number one and do not begin number two until number one is finished. I have to use this same technique in my life. There are things that I do not like to do and one of these is to put the suitcases in the attic after we have returned from a trip. I usually let them set at the door and finally go make myself put them away. The way that I do this is to simply say, "Look, it will take thirty seconds to take these suitcases up there to the attic, set them down, and be finished." Often I have had to say, "Go." This is a matter of discipline.

When we do these tasks separately and individually, as I have suggested, then we can do them in a systematic, orderly way, and will feel a sense of accomplishment. We are also telling our spouses we enjoy our homes, and want to take part in it and be involved with the home itself. Take time for tasks.

These tasks should not all be delegated to the husband or to the wife. The children need to be taught that they have responsibilities. Assign duties to the children daily. This may involve making the beds, cleaning their rooms, vacuuming, carrying out the trash, mowing the yard, cleaning up the kitchen, preparing the meal, or any other particular responsibility. If they use the car, then they should have the responsibility of seeing that it is kept clean, so this would mean washing it. The children should learn that there is more to life than getting home from school, jumping on their bikes, and riding all afternoon. Teach them that they have obligations and responsibilities as part of the family.

Teamwork

When we view marriage it must be viewed as a partnership. This simply means partners work together as a team. I suppose that the idea of teamwork came from the athletic contests where a group of people work together toward the same goal and the same victory. Those of you with an agricultural background may think of a team of mules harnessed together and working together. When they pull together the work is easy. If one pulls and the other does not, then the job will not be done as quickly. So, we need to take time for teamwork. Ask yourself, "Are we really working together? Do we have goals that are the same and reasonable objectives that each of us knows about?"

In many families the husband waits for the wife to make the decisions, or the wife will not do anything until the husband tells her to do it. Soon the relationship becomes that of slave and slave master, boss and servant, or employer and employee. The family is a team. Children need both parents to rear, train, and direct them. The husband needs to know that the wife is working with him, and the wife needs to know that the husband is interested in what she is doing and working with her also.

Partnership in marriage will certainly mean a better relationship in marriage. This is not contradictory to New Testament teaching. I believe it fits well with the principle where the Lord said, "The husband is the head of the wife" (Eph. 5:23). The idea of being the head does not mean "me master, you slave." We are a part of each other and I have a responsibility to you and I am willing to assume it. I will take the lead in providing for your well-being and my well-being and will do all I can do to benefit us. It means that we are a team and a part of each other. It means when decisions are made the wife considers the husband and the husband considers the wife. It is a partnership throughout—deep concern for one another. Take time for teamwork.

In order to work together couples have to talk together, plan together, and discuss objectives and goals together. It is impossible to take time for teamwork unless you have taken time to talk.

Teen-agers

I am sure that you are well aware that for each of these segments of the word *time* and the letter *T*, a book could be written. My purpose is to give you some ideas to think about and then you can develop them further. Taking time for teen-agers is extremely important. The family teaches us economic skills, our attitude toward work, the art of financial independence, our money habits, and our family habits. The family is a much stronger teacher of the fundamental future skills of an individual than is any other educational process that we know of. The family is even a stronger teacher of religion and religious ideals than the church is. For it is in the family that the child sees religion in practice every day rather than just hearing about it once a week. By spending time with teen-agers you are strengthening the family, and remember that whatever strengthens the family strengthens society. When you have children you are assuming a tremendous responsibility. You have created another human being and have passed from one part of your life to another. There was a time when you were a child, but now you are an adult and have accepted the responsibility of rearing your children.

The importance of taking time to be with teen-agers cannot be explained in such a short space, nor do I have the vocabulary or the ability to impress it on you as certainly as it should be impressed. These young people, your children, are looking to you for guidance. As they have been growing up you should have been spending time with them. Now that they are in the teen years it is even more important to continue this association with them. When you are spending time with your teen-ager you are there to supervise, direct, and show him you are interested in him. You become aware of his thoughts, ideals, goals, and aims. Teens do not seem so distant if you spend time with them.

Newsweek magazine stated in 1975 that the average father spends less than fifteen minutes per day with a child. Fathers, this is not enough time to motivate, direct, and really show your children that you are interested in them. The same article stated that the average mother spends less than twenty minutes per day with her children. The same thing is true here in that this small amount of time is not sufficient to direct and train your children.

These years in the life of a teen-ager are critical.

23

It is now that teens are thinking of occupations and goals for life. They need to be taught responsibility and be prepared for the time when they will manage their own money, their own time, and their own lives. Taking time with them will help you share your experiences with them and help them make a decision about the type of occupation that will be most beneficial to them and that will fit their temperament.

Spending time with your teens will help you become acquainted with their friends. You need to know with whom they are associating. You need to know where they are going, what they are doing, and what time they will be home. By spending time with them you will know when they come in at night. Every mother and father should be up or awake when their children come in at night. This is spending time with your teenagers.

We live in a time when the motor bike has given to the teen-ager mobility beyond imagination. In a matter of minutes the child can be five or ten miles away from home. The parents really have no contact with them. It is sad that many parents turn their children loose every evening and the children go anywhere they please. Parents, you need to spend time with your teen-agers. Father, do not expect your wife to do all this, and mother, do not expect your husband to do all this by himself. The responsibility of taking time for teen-agers is the responsibility of both mothers and fathers.

A television station ran an announcement each evening at ten o'clock and the question was, "Parents do you know where your children are?" The station decided to call various homes about this time and make a random survey to see how well this question was being received. To the interviewers' surprise, they found they should have turned the question around and asked, "Children, do you know where your parents are?" The interviewers found that many parents were not at home and the children were. Parents, you can become so involved in your social and business life that you do not know your children because you are not spending time with them.

The argument against this is usually, "If I spend time with them then I won't have any time for myself. I don't think that children should demand all my time." I can certainly appreciate this attitude, but let me point out several things. First, the children will not be with you for that long. In all probability you will have the direction of the children for seventeen, eighteen, or nineteen years and then they will be gone from home. They will be in college, married, or out in the world by themselves. At this time you will be about forty-five years old or possibly fifty. In all probability your children will live away from home for more years then they will live at home. Second, when you decided to have children you should have known whether you were mature enough to have children, and that children meant responsibility. They did not ask to come into the world. You brought the child into the world. At that time, you were saying by your actions, "We want to have a child to rear, to train, to love, to make our family complete." Certainly you should have known that it would take time to be with the children and time to enjoy the children.

Spending time with children will be the greatest joy that you can experience if you start early in life and let that continue through the teen-age years and the years when your children have their own families.

Temper

There will be times when you are frustrated, upset, and irritated. So you need to have a time for temper. You need to have a time to get all of your frustrations out of your system.

You can control your temper, and it is not necessary for you to go through life without raising your voice or never expressing hostility about anything. Do not just "swallow hard" and turn your anger all to the inside. This is bad for your body.

You need time for temper or time for arguments. There is a fine series of verses in Ephesians. Paul said, "Be ye angry, and sin not: let not the sun go down upon your wrath. . . . Let all bitterness, and wrath, and anger, and clamour, and evil speaking, be put away from you, with all malice; And be ye kind one to another, tenderhearted, forgiving one another, even as God for Christ's sake hath forgiven you." (Eph. 4:26, 31–32). Another passage, James 1:19, says, "Be swift to hear, slow to speak, slow to wrath." You do need a time to express your anger.

I would suggest that any arguments or disagreement between you and your spouse should follow the rules about how to argue. Very briefly, these rules are:

1. Argue once per day, no more than thirty minutes, about one subject only.
2. You may not bring up any unpleasant subject that happened more than two weeks ago.
3. You may not argue and express your temper one hour after arising in the morning or two hours before bedtime.
4. If you express your temper you may shout, as

long as you cannot be heard outside your house, and no other people are present.
5. You may argue and express your temper so long as there is no violence or profanity.
6. You may not express your temper and argue at mealtimes.
7. The temper and argument should not continually be expressed in front of the children. It is not damaging to have normal friction expressed in front of the children. However, they should not be exposed to a steady diet of mother's and daddy's temper tantrums and arguments.
8. Take time for temper.

Our emotions have been created within us and these emotions need expression. I sometimes compare emotion with a carbonated beverage. When we put a finger on the top of the bottle and shake it, the gas expands and the liquid spews out. As we become more and more frustrated, the emotions build up. We need to take time and get them out.

Travel

For a marriage to be enjoyable, and to break your routine, I recommend that you travel together. Nearly every company offers its employees paid vacations every year. I am amazed at the number of people who never take these vacations. It is not unusual for clients to tell me that they have not been on a vacation for five, ten, or even twenty years.

Traveling together can be an exciting time that brings the family together in a closer relationship by doing fun things. In order to make travel an enjoyable thing, do not make the mistake of starting on a 700-mile trip and believe that you must drive straight through and not make any stops. Children traveling in a car cannot sit still for fifteen, eighteen, or twenty hours. They become irritable and you become irritable as all of you get tired. Half of the fun is getting there. Limit your travel to six to eight hours a day. Stop early in motels so the children can play and relax. Your traveling time will become enjoyment time for your family. Your children will be able to look back over the years and remember the good times with mother and daddy. If you drive endless hours and everybody gets tired, irritable, fussy, and extremely unhappy, then the next time a vacation is scheduled it will not be a pleasant, exciting outing at all.

Traveling together means that you are giving memories to your family that will be with them for the rest of their lives. Travel means you expose them to educational situations—the past happenings of our nation. It means you show them different parts of the country.

I recommend that families take mini-vacations, three-day and four-day vacations. The tremendous increase in outdoor facilities for camping means that families can go more often with less expense than otherwise. Parents, take time to travel witt your family.

Taking time for travel is also good advice for you as husbands and wives when the children leave home. We have a tendency to get in a rut and do the same things every day. As husband and wife, when the children are gone, you need to take time to be together and spend weekends away from the normal routine. In my practice as a clinician in marriage and family counseling, I have found that couples who get away for short trips have opportunities to talk together, enjoy each other, and get away from the daily responsibilities that may be adding pressures to their already-difficult lives.

Trouble

One of the writers of the Old Testament said, "Man that is born of woman is full of troubles." There has never been a time when any of us has not known some sort of difficulty. It seems that as soon as we get one problem worked out, another starts. The soap operas we see on television are very true to life. About the time one climax works out and seems to be settling down, the writers introduce another character and you begin to see how another crisis is going to be developed.

In every life there will be troubles and difficulties. These troubles will be of every kind. There will be times when our health will not be the best, or we will not have enough money, or our family will be disappointing us, or there will be job pressures. What will you do with these troubles? Take time for them. First, realize that your troubles are there and that they are real. Secondly, after defining them, try to seek a possible solution. Third, as soon as you have done all that you possibly can, lay your problem aside for another view a little bit later. Fourth, realize that many troubles will have to run the course.

I doubt that there is any way that you can foresee all the troubles that you will have and take precautions against them. For the financial problems that may face you, I suggest that you have at least three to five months of savings to live on in the event the unexpected arises.

There are going to be troubles in our lives but most of our troubles come from our own neglect and not looking ahead. By spending time talking together, meeting your tasks together, and working together, you will be better able to face any troubles that may come later in life. If the troubles you are facing seem too much for both of you and seem to be breaking up your family, seek professional help. That professional help may be legal, medical, psychological, or religious. But do seek help if the troubles you have are much greater than you are able to bear.

3
Time For "I"

If you were writing this book you would probably do exactly as I have in introducing "I" with the concept of intimacy.

Intimacy

Have you really thought of why you married and why you wanted a family? You had been dating for a time and decided that you wanted to live with this person for the rest of your life. You had a desire to be intimate with him or her not only sexually, but also emotionally, intellectually, and socially. It may seem strange that I suggest that you should take time for intimacy, but this is absolutely necessary. In dealing with hundreds of couples in marriage and family counseling, I have found that too few of them take time for their intimate relationship, their sex relationship. There must be time for physical togetherness.

When God created man He created us male and female. I believe it is interesting to note that the Bible never uses the word *sex* but always refers to gender.

This is because the two genders are opposites and attract one another. Therefore, there is to be an attraction of the male to the female. God created us with this attraction to the opposite sex. However, the way that one uses this intimacy can mean a great deal to one's partner or be very degrading. Take time for intimacy. One's relationship with his spouse is not just a five- or ten-minute contact once or twice a day. The intimate relationship, the sexual relationship, is a result of a mental relationship and emotional involvement much earlier in the day. I have often stated that sex begins in the kitchen, in the living room, in the yard, in the car as we are talking, and finally is consummated at a later time. Too often, in dealing with troubled couples, I have found that one partner leaves the impression with the spouse that the physical relationship is all he wants and that he does not care for the person as a whole. He or she is interested in the sex relationship and does not care about the husband or wife outside of this intimacy.

In order to take time for intimacy, let me suggest that you take time for talking. This was discussed in detail in the previous chapter. Second, let me suggest that you both retire about the same time. It is not unusual for me to find couples who never retire at the same time. One may retire early and one may stay up late. These people never are in bed together to talk and build up to their relationship. Third, time for intimacy means that there is time for being together. Often I recommend that couples spend at least thirty minutes per day in listening to music and merely sitting and talking. This is a form of intimacy. So many people make the statement, "I would just like to be held." There is the need on the part of each of us to be held. We think about times when we pick up a little child in our arms and hold him close to us. It seems that the child realizes that we care and are concerned. Children can sense this warmth for them as we hold them. This same thing is true in adults. There must be a time when spouses just hold each other and talk to one another.

Taking time for intimacy then will let one's spouse know that one is interested in the other not merely as a sex object but as a whole individual—the complete person. Otherwise, if we have no contact with our spouses outside the sex relationship, they soon get the idea that this is the only purpose for having married them.

Taking time for intimacy means that we continue to date one another. You are involved with your spouse, endeavoring to please and "make brownie points" when you are dating.

I realize that in this book I cannot really touch all areas but it is important to understand that intimacy is an important part of marriage. We generally think of intimacy as the sex relationship. However, I like to think of intimacy as not only sex but also as conversing, traveling, buying, eating, being together, listening to music together, attending things together, and rearing children together. All of these involve times for intimacy, time for being with the one that you selected as your lifelong mate. This is intimacy.

Infants

It seems axiomatic that the time for infants would immediately follow the time for intimacy. We do know that as a result of intimacy, children will be born. This is the way God created us and this is a very natural result of intimacy. But I need to emphasize that we must take time for infants. One of the great beauties of family life is the birth of a child. I hope that your attitude about children is not like that of a young woman who said to me, "I wouldn't mind having children but, you know, when you have children you have them forever."

When a husband and wife are in love and this love brings into being a child, they have presented to the world a part of themselves. When the movement of new life is felt within the mother then there is a great sense of maturity and a great sense of contributing to life itself. Also, there is the overwhelming thought of the responsibility of directing this child. This new life that is coming into the world will be completely dependent on the generosity and wisdom of its parents. As parents you will be passing on to another generation a part of yourself. You will be relaying to another generation a part of your ideals, a part of your temperament, a part of you. Often the fact that you have given birth to a child means a part of you will never die. Thus you have become part of the great chain of things in life. You become the link between ancestors and heirs. As you hold this little child in your arms, you probably recognize just how helpless the child is. You should also realize how responsible you must be in directing this child, helping and encouraging this child in the years to come.

You must take time for your infant. Fathers have a difficult role put on them now. In every culture and society that we know anything about, the mother gives birth to a child and then the father goes out and forages for food. He comes back and takes care of the helpless female while she takes care of the helpless child. Then about the time the child grows a little and the mother can expend her energies in a different way, she is pregnant again and gives birth to another child, which means the male then has the obligation of supporting another child while the female is caring for the helpless child. Thus, the family unit is locked in due to the helplessness of the child. There is no other created being that has a family-unit structure like that of the human family.

As parents, we have obligations. One's obligation as a father is that of earning a living, supporting the family, but at the same time being a husband and father. Spending time with your infant means that you will be with the child as much as possible. It means that both parents will know how to change diapers, both of you will be able to feed the child, both of you will be able to be up at night with the child, both of you will walk and rock your child. It means further that both of you will play with your child, read to him, and let him know that you are an integral part of him. As a parent you may think your children are taking too much of your time, and you are no longer free to do what you want to do. Many families have solved this by hiring baby sitters or putting the child in a day-care home and then going about what they please to do. They leave the training of the most precious possession that they have, and the most precious thing that forms the future of the world, to someone who is less skilled and talented and interested than they are. We must take time for our infants.

Time will pass rather rapidly. In a few years we will look back on the early years with our children and we will wonder where the time has gone. We will regret not having been with our children when they learned to crawl, took their first steps, said their first words, and began to explore many things that excite them. If you do not spend time with your infants you will miss the greatest experiences that you will ever know. It is difficult to tell you what it means to see the excitement of a child as he sees for the first time a tree, or a leaf, or a bird, or even is able to tell you where his eye is. This is your child and you brought this child into the world. Spend time with your infant.

Sometimes couples are so selfish about their own lives that they don't want to be bothered with their infants. Therefore, the husband and the wife keep account of the time that they spend with the child and endeavor to make the other one spend as much time with the child as he or she did. Parents should enjoy spending time with their infants.

Even at early ages the infants can learn from us. It is in these early months that we begin the training and set the pattern of the life for this child that will go with him for the balance of his life on this earth. Take time for your infant.

In-laws

In nearly every marriage, because of the nature of the marriage laws themselves, there are those whom we refer to as in-laws. Some people have stated they are more like out-laws but, be that as it may, the parents of your spouse fit into your family picture. When you marry, you marry her parents and you marry his parents. Also, you marry his brothers and sisters and her brothers and sisters. Therefore, it is certainly important that you take time for in-laws.

It is not wise for the in-laws to dominate your family life, nor is it wise to exclude the in-laws from your family life. You need to realize that they have their families and you are now a separate family entirely. Sometimes parents demand that their married children see them every week, have certain meals with them every week, take vacations together, and so on. As parents we must realize that our children are now established in their own homes, have their own lifestyles, and have their own goals. We must respect them as another family unit. So, we deal with them as adults. It is important that we visit with our children and that we continue to enjoy our children even after they are married. Taking time for in-laws means that we continue friendly, social, enjoyable relationships.

When I discuss in-laws, I am aware that this introduces several other dimensions of the family. As parents, we see our married children possibly making mistakes or seeming mistakes, and therefore we try to inject our advice. My recommendation is that in-laws should not offer advice until they are asked.

Taking time for in-laws does not mean that you report daily to your parents as to what you are doing, where you are going, and where you have been. But it does mean that you continue to treat your parents with respect, with kindness, and as friends. As in-laws they will be the grandparents. Your children need to have the opportunity of associating with their grandparents and grandparents need to have the pleasure of associating with their grandchildren. However, you should not expect the grandparents to rear your children because you do not want to be bothered with childrearing. I do understand that there are times of economic necessity when grandparents can assist in rearing children. It is bad if you make the decision that you do not want to take care of the infants and therefore you let the in-laws, the grandparents, rear them for you.

Idleness

You may think it is strange that I suggest that there be a time for idleness—just doing nothing. I heard a busy executive say that someone called him once and asked him what he was planning to do on a certain day. He responded, "I am not planning to do anything that day." The man said, "Well, fine. We will be happy to have you come to speak to us. You will be able to come." The executive replied, "No, I said I was not doing anything that day. I am just going to do nothing." His idea was that there is a time when we really do nothing. I am well aware that some of you are going to say, "That is for me. I just want to do nothing." I do not mean that idleness should be taken to the extreme where we never do anything. There must be a time when we stop and do nothing. Stop and meditate. Stop and think.

We all lead busy lives. It seems as though our entire lives are geared to the minute hand on the clock. We punch the clock when we go to work or we work strictly by appointment. Our time is governed by the clock. So we are always busy. We need time to sit down and think. Some major organizations have realized the necessity of time to think, so they have what they call think tanks. The executives do nothing but think and talk. Yes, you need to take time to be idle—time to do nothing, a time to think, a time to let your mind take flights of fancy. You need times of idleness.

In the Old Testament one of the writers says, "Be still and know that I am God." Even there Divinity was saying, "Stop. Be still. Do nothing. Begin to think. Realize." I do suggest that there must be a time when husband and wife can merely sit down and do nothing and be with each other, a time to be by themselves and think. So there needs to be a time for idleness.

Improvement

There are none of us who cannot improve. But many of us stop improving when we finish high school or college. There must be a time for improvement. In order to do this let me suggest two means for improving yourself. First, read good educational books. Second, continue adult education.

Improvement means that we can improve our social lives, our business lives, our minds, our manners, our vocabularies and our attitudes. Someone has said that the biggest room in the world is the room for improvement.

Take time to improve your family life. You are going to get out of your home and family only that which you put in it. It is strange that so many businessmen buy books and take courses to improve their capacity as executives, but they do not expend the same amount of time and energy on learning how to be a better husband.

Many wives do not concentrate on how to be a better wife. Wives and mothers can improve on cooking, housekeeping, decorating, training the children, or gardening.

All of these things I have mentioned, for both husbands and wives, are vital to either life or both lives. There is room for improvement. As parents you should endeavor to expose your children to some of the finer things of life. See that they have opportunities to appreciate good music, speakers, books, art and sculpture, foods, and associates. Take time for improvements in your family life.

4
Time For "M"

Meals

To some people, it may seem peculiar that I suggest that you take time for meals, but it is very important. This is a time when all the family should be able to sit down, eat together, and enjoy a pleasant relationship. I have found that few families sit down together every day. In some homes where there are children, each child eats at a separate time and the mother and father do not even eat together. This means that the family does not get together as a unit every day.

While lecturing at a high school, I asked the students how many of them had sat down at the table with all of the members of their family and had a meal together in the last week. When the hands were raised, the response showed that fewer than 25 percent of the families sat down for a meal together during the last 168 hours. In our active society this is one of the tragedies that we live with. The father's working hours do not necessarily make it convenient and all the outside activities do not necessarily make it easy for the children to be home at the same time. However, it is important that we take time for meals. Mothers, this will mean that you set a definite time for meals and work toward having meals ready at that time. Husbands, this means that you make every effort to be home at that time. Children, this means that you make every effort possible to be home at that time. I realize there will be extenuating circumstances that will keep you from being home when meals are ready. However, it should be the unusual rather than the usual.

Mealtimes should be pleasant times. This is a time when the entire family can be around the table at the same time and enjoy a relaxed atmosphere. Parents should see that arguments are not carried on at the table and conversation should be as agreeable as possible. Parents, this is a time when you should not be at your highest level of hostility. These guidelines mean that mealtime will be enjoyable.

Taking time for meals also means that the meals are planned. I know that it becomes difficult to plan meals that everybody always likes, but here is where the training of children comes in. You should prepare food that is good for the children and prepare it in such a way that it will be appetizing. It is not wise for parents merely to prepare food that their children like. If your children do not like certain foods you need to teach them to like those foods and develop an appetite for them. It is a sad mistake to let children eat only what they like and not sample various kinds of food.

Taking time for meals will mean that you have a leisurely meal, a time when you can sit at the table and discuss what has happened during the day or the things that you are planning to do.

Mealtime is a time when you as a family can come

together and again receive nurture from one another as members of the same unit. To the best of your ability, see that mealtimes are pleasant.

See that children are prepared for the meal by being clean and having stopped play long enough before the meal so they will be calm when they are ready to sit down and eat. Mealtime should be a pleasant time and a time for all to be together. Take time for meals.

Manners

It is in connection with meals that I suggest manners because it is at mealtime that you can teach your children proper manners. This means that you teach them how to hold their knives and forks, how to set the table properly, what to do with their napkins, how to take food onto their plates, how to chew, how to conduct themselves at the table, and general rules of good etiquette. Some people may ask why this is necessary. It is necessary because the children will not be eating at home all of their lives but will be out in public. Certainly you will want them to know how to conduct themselves in public so that they will be using good manners.

Taking time for manners also means that as parents we take time for courtesy to each other. I mean opening doors, holding coats, assisting another if visibility is poor, and performing any other acts of kindness. Manners are important because they affect our relationships with other people.

I encourage parents to teach their children manners, not only those that apply to eating but also especially those relating to adults. A woman once remarked, after hearing one of my lectures about parent-child relationships, "I wish you would put into your lecture the idea of teaching children to speak to adults.

Not long back," she continued, "I went into a room where there were children and spoke to them. They just looked at me. They never said a word. They never responded to my greeting." This is certainly an area that parents need to teach children about—how to display good manners to an adult or to their elders.

Good manners involve using a respectful tone of voice, responding to what the adults have said, talking to them, and respecting them because they are older. Taking time for manners means that we are training our children for the interrelationships in which they are going to live.

There is another area of manners that I could spend hundreds of pages on, but I can only touch on it here. Parents, do you realize how cruel children can be? Try to work with them on their attitudes toward other children and on using good manners in their peer group. It is sad when children refer to other children who wear glasses as "four eyes," or find some other seeming peculiarity and make fun of it. How many times have you heard children called "buck tooth," "skinny," "fatty," "bowlegged," "big ears," or other names? These things hurt! As parents you oftentimes hear these statements made and pass them off as being just childishness. Remember, children have feelings, and good manners on the part of your child require that he does not look at other children and make fun of their seeming peculiarities. I am afraid too many people have watched television programs that are geared primarily to cutting, sarcastic, and belittling remarks of the "All in the Family" style. Good manners mean that I am concerned with the feelings of the other person and that I want "to do unto others as I would have them do unto me."

Moods

As human beings we are all susceptible to moods. In a good family and marriage situation, I will be aware of the moods of my spouse. Let us consider the mood of the husband when he comes in after having had a difficult day. Suppose that he has told his wife about the difficulties that he is having at work. She should be aware of the mood that he is in and be as supportive as possible. It is not wise to take the side of his antagonist and let him believe that he not only has to fight those at the office but also has to fight his wife because she believes he is wrong. When he is "down in the dumps" she can be empathetic.

Husbands, be aware of the moods of your wives. We know that the female is more susceptible to moodiness, because of her biological make-up, than the male. Due to the menstrual cycle there will be certain times of the month, as her body changes, when her moodiness will be more apparent than at other times. There is not a great deal that she can do about this. She knows it is going to come and you know that it is going to come. Therefore, adjust and modify your behavior to fit her moods. I often recommend that you chart yourselves every month. The charting should be done on the basis of 0–10, letting 0 stand for depression or a very low mood and 10 stand for happiness or a very high mood. If you will do this consistently for several months, marking every day what the attitudes are, then you will realize that these moods come at certain times of the month.

Also, moods come as a result of other pressures in and outside the family. When your husband or wife needs kindness and assistance, be there with your spouse. A woman who had lost a relative told me, "You know, at no time did he [her husband] ever come up and just put his arms around me and say, 'Honey, I am sorry.' It seems as though I was having to bear it all by myself." The idea is that we must be aware of the mood of the other person. There are times when our spouses do not want to talk. I would suggest that at this time the one who is in the deep mood and wants to be left alone should tell his spouse. You could say, "Honey, I am down and don't feel well. I would like to be by myself for a little while."

In one case I dealt with several years ago, the man had a bad habit of pouting. I had to go to extremes to break this habit but I finally suggested that he put a little card on his chair so that others would see what his mood was. On this card he was to write, "I am pouting. Leave me alone." After he had done that two or three times and it became rather ridiculous and funny, he realized that pouting is not a mood that is acceptable in the family for an extended time.

Take time for the moods of your family. When family members are happy, be happy with them. One of the basic teachings of the Bible is "weep with them that weep, mourn with them that mourn, laugh with them that laugh." If part of my body is happy the rest of my body should be happy also. This is how we are connected in the family—as a part of the body itself. Be susceptible to moods. If you want to cry and crying helps relieve tension, then cry. Let others express their moods in this particular way. I do not mean that the crying should go on for weeks and weeks and months and months. I do mean that when a wife, husband, or child desires to express his mood with tears, then let him do this without making fun of him or making him feel guilty. Let him know that you are understanding, concerned, and interested.

Taking time for the moods of your spouse will certainly mean that you take time to talk with him or her. The worst thing you could possibly say is "snap out of it." Do not give the impression that you are not interested in him or her and what has been happening. Let your spouse know that you are interested and will sit down and help in any way possible.

Some people have suggested the way to handle the moods of one's spouse is to leave him or her alone. This only compounds the loneliness and frustration that is there anyway.

The word *mood* also applies to enthusiasm. If the children have excelled or the husband or wife has excelled in something, be happy with that person. Enjoy his success with him. Don't be a wet blanket about the things he has accomplished. When the children have made good marks or have excelled and received a trophy, enjoy their success with them. Let them know that you are as happy about it as they are. Take time to enjoy the moods of your family.

Money

There are two things that I want to mention in connection with time in a good marriage. This one is taking time for money and the next will be taking time for management.

I do realize that money is important. Someone has said that "money is not number one but number two is so far behind it that it is hard to know what it is." This may be a rather ridiculous way to put it, but money is important. Money is a means of exchange that is accepted nationwide. I trade my time and services for money. Then I trade that money for another person's time and services. So money is a vital part of life.

Taking time for money does not mean that we let money be the all-consuming objective and goal of life itself. It is not uncommon for me to hear a couple say that they are interested in making money. "Our goal is to have lots of money. We want to have $200,000 in just a few years. This becomes their all-consuming goal. This is taking too much time for money. Another way to say it is, they are taking all of their time for money and they soon have no time for the family. We need to take time for money, yes, but we need to keep money in its proper perspective.

Regularly I require my clients to write. There is a reason for this. They need to get their thoughts on paper. I suggest that you write down your goals and objectives in life. If all of your goals are surrounded by dollar signs, then you need to change your goals and objectives a little.

How much time do you spend earning a living? A young man once told me that he was making $500 a week and he was thrilled with this. I certainly did appreciate the fact that he was earning that much, but I was disappointed to find out that in order for him to earn that, he was working nearly ninety hours per week. This left practically no time at home for his family.

Taking time for money means that we will do that which is required of us to earn our living but it also means that we will enjoy our money and our families for whom we are working.

Taking time for money also means that we take the time to teach our children the use of money and the value of it. We will encourage them to live within an allowance and begin making decisions early in life as to the things that are important to buy. Taking time for money means that we will earn it and enjoy it.

Management

I believe it wise to discuss management with money because the two are so closely connected. Anybody can earn money but it takes a person who really puts time and thought to it to manage money. In fact, management can affect every particular aspect of life itself.

Taking time to manage your money means taking time to spend it wisely, invest it wisely, save it wisely, and use it to the wisest and fullest extent.

Management means that we learn to pay our bills on time and that we try to stay away from high interest and carrying charges.

Management means that we buy those things that are durable rather those things that merely have a low price. Management means that we look seriously at a bargain to see whether it *is* a bargain.

Taking time for management also means that we take time to manage our time. Many of us waste so much time and it is the most precious commodity that we have. I often recommend that a person analyze his activities for a period of several weeks by writing down what he is doing each hour of each day. It will surprise you how much time you waste when you could be doing things that are genuinely important.

Taking time to manage household activities and even to do your grocery shopping and yard work is important. These items have to do with the home and the house. Taking time to plan a meal will cut down on expenses. Taking time for planning yard work will also help you get more done.

Management then means that we look at the family and at the home as a business, as a partnership, and as a profit-making organization in which the profit is enjoyment, pleasure, and fulfillment.

Marriage

It is sad that I even have to say, "Take time to be married." All I am saying is that you need to take time to be a husband and a wife, a mother and a father. Taking time for marriage means taking time to be together, talk together, travel together, go out together, rear the children together, and in general spend time together. If you do not want to spend time with your husband or wife, then you should not have married.

When a couple comes to marry they are telling each other and the world that they are going to live together, work together, play together, and be together for the rest of their lives. That is going to take time.

5
Time For "E"

Encouragement

It may sound odd to some of you that I have to suggest that couples take time to encourage one another. But this is absolutely necessary. In many families the husband never makes a complimentary, ego-boosting statement to his wife and she never says anything that makes him feel important. Encouragement simply means that a person, by what he or she says and does, gives a spouse courage to go on positively and progressively. Taking time for encouragement means that we will take time to see what our spouses are doing and that we will take time to compliment and comment on their activities.

One of the greatest things you can say is, "Thank you." Another phrase you can use is, "I appreciate you" (or, "it," whatever the situation might be). It certainly would not hurt us to turn to our mates sometime and say, "You know, I appreciate you." We need to take time for encouragement.

Day by day our tasks and our routines become monotonous and the monotony can be broken only by the rewards of payday or the rewards of somebody saying, "Well done."

I appreciate the fact that the Bible refers to the judgment in a dual sense, in that we have a goal for which we are working. That goal is heaven. But also the Bible says that at judgment the statement will be made, "Well done, thou good and faithful servant." In other words, at the end of our lives the comment will be, "You have done a good job; therefore, here is the reward." In our married lives it is good if we say to each other, "I appreciate you; I like what you are doing; you are doing a good job," or whatever the situation calls for. Take time for encouragement.

You might refer to encouragement as positive motivation. That is exactly what it is. We all like to be complimented for what we have done, and whether we call it a compliment or not, we like to have people notice that we have done something. It is certainly encouraging when someone says, "I like what you have done. I appreciate what you have done." It is meaningful. We need to encourage others.

So often I hear my clients say that they want their spouses to express appreciation for them. This is why I am including this section.

The Bible tells a beautiful story that I have titled "Breaking the Alabaster Box." This story is recorded in Mark 14:3–9. The interesting statement from this story is when the Lord said, "She hath done what she could." As Mark writes, a woman had come and anointed Jesus' body with oil. Those standing around said it was a waste of money because they could have sold the oil for 300 pence and given that money to the poor. So they criticized her severely for wasting this oil on the Lord. He said, "Let her alone . . . she has wrought a good work on me." Actually what He was saying is that she had expressed her appreciation. She had told Me how much she cares for Me, and she was encouraging Me. This is taking time to show affection, taking time to show concern, taking time to show your love and appreciation.

The idea of taking time for encouragement certainly is applicable to our treatment of our children. Many men and women work very effectively with other people's children, in Scouts or church youth groups, but do not spend a great deal of time encouraging their own children. We need to take time to encourage our children.

A father wanted to encourage his son but in the illustration that I am going to present, he did it poorly. The young man had played baseball that day and had made two mistakes. Going home from the ball game, the father told his child that he would have to spend at least two hours in his room thinking about why he had made such errors. This was not encouragement. The father defended his action by saying, "I wanted him to think about why he made the mistakes and do better next time." On the surface this seems like a rational point but the father's action was punishment to the child because the errors could possibly have been just normal reactions or improper reactions. This was not encouragement.

A mother wanted to encourage her child to do better because he was failing in school. Her supposed encouragement was, "Son, let's try to do a little bit better the next time." This was not encouragement. This was almost apathy on her part. Encouragement would have been taking time to find out why he had not been studying, why his study habits were so poor, and becoming interested long before the grade period was ended. Encouraging your children means letting them know you love them, have a concern for them, and are interested in spending time with them.

I want to expand the idea of encouragement to include encouraging your children to continue their education. When parents take education seriously there is the probability the children will take it seriously also. But if the children see that the parents do not care and the parents are not showing a real interest, then the schools cannot work as effectively. I believe parents should study various things in order to help their children.

Recently I noticed some statistics on unemployment. Now this is an area where you can talk to your children intelligently about figures that are in black and white. It might be wise to show your children tables in which the Bureau of Labor Statistics presented unemployment by occupation. The lowest unemployment was in the area of proprietors and managers. The next was in professional and technical and the next was in sales work. Unemployment began to increase for clerical workers and skilled workers but unemployment was greatest among semiskilled and unskilled workers. This simply means that those who have no skills or those who have few skills are the first ones out of work. To encourage your child in education means to sit down and talk to him about the skills that are necessary to support his family in years to come.

Entertainment and Enjoyment

Would you be embarrassed if I asked you and your family a simple question? The question is, "What do you do for fun?" Many of you would have difficulty in answering. Many would say, "We do not do anything for fun. As a family we never do anything or go anywhere just for fun." This is tragic. Think about the reason for a family and home: it is so two people can be together for the balance of their lives and serve as helpmeets for each other. We should enjoy being together. When our children are born, we should be with them and enjoy them. In fact, the whole purpose of the family as God described it, founded it, and created it in the Garden of Eden, was that man should not be alone. My question then again is, "Do you take time for entertainment and enjoyment?"

Entertainment should be such that the family can be involved in it. A lot of times we plan our hobbies, athletic events, or entertainment so that it involves only "me." If I have entertainment at the expense of my family's boredom, this is not helping the family. There are myriads of golf widows, tennis widows, hunting widows, fishing widows, or business widows because men are happy in their work or recreation, receiving their entertainment there. But what about the wives? They, having been involved with the children, seek adult entertainment with their husbands.

Husband and wives, do you plan your entertainment together? I certainly encourage the wives to be involved with their husbands in athletic activities, fishing, or other activities, at least as much as possible. This does not mean all of our entertainment is what one wants to do to the exclusion of the other's desires. It does mean that in entertainment we decide what both of us want to do. It also means that I taper and change my taste so I can enjoy what my spouse enjoys. Together, we can enjoy those things.

In some circumstances, for instance, one of the couple likes opera, ballet, or other classical music. The spouse does not care for this. For a good marriage, the spouse would attend, and who knows, might begin to learn to enjoy it. By the way, if you do go with your spouse and you do not like that type of entertainment, do not sigh, grumble, and complain the entire evening. It would have been better that you had stayed at home. However, it is best to change your attitude and go with him or her at that particular time. So, how much time do you take for entertainment and enjoyment?

Taking time for entertainment and enjoyment means playing games with your children and being involved with them. Sometimes parents say, "Mr. Jerkins, I'm just not a game player." As parents, you should realize that your children do play games and this is a fine way for them to learn. It is also a fine way to get better acquainted and more closely involved with them. Therefore, I strongly suggest that you share entertainment and enjoyment with your children. The games that you play will be simple ones and I am sure may be boring to you. Remember, as you are taking time for entertainment, you are with your children and show them that you are genuinely interested in them.

Taking time for entertainment means that when the children grow up you get involved in things outside the home with them. Little boys like to play ball and get involved in other sports, so parents need to be out with them. Notice that I said parents, plural, and that was certainly no mistake. Little girls, as they get older, get involved in outside activities. Again, both parents need to take time for entertainment with them.

Marriage should be fun and enjoyable and exciting. But you cannot merely wait around for fun to come. You have to put something into marriage itself. Take time for fun, entertainment, and enjoyment.

Equality

You may be startled that I say that you need to take time for equality. Read with me a series of verses from the Bible that presents this idea, and you will better appreciate it. "Wives, submit yourself unto your own husbands, as unto the Lord. For the husband is the head of the wife, even as Christ is the head of the church: and he is the saviour of the body. Therefore as the church is subject unto Christ, so let the wives be to their own husbands in every thing. Husbands, love your wives, even as Christ also loved the church, and gave himself for it; . . . So ought men to love their wives as their own bodies. He that loveth his wife loveth himself. For no man ever yet hated his own flesh; but nourisheth and cherisheth it, even as the Lord the church: For we are members of his body, of his flesh, and of his bones. For this cause shall a man leave his father and mother, and shall be joined unto his wife, and they two shall be one flesh. . . . Nevertheless let every one of you in particular so love his wife even as himself; and the wife see that she reverence her husband" (Eph. 5:22–33). The Bible is simply teaching that the husband and wife are part of each other. Look at your body now. Can you think of a particular part of your body that is more important than any other? Would you like to do away with your hands, your arms, your feet, or your head? Would you be willing to give up your stomach, your liver, or your heart?

It is in the same way that the Lord said husbands and wives are a part of each other. We are a part of each other, exactly as the different organs of the body make up the body itself. This is why I say take time for equality. We are a part of the same body.

If couples really believe that they are a part of each other, it would do away with one of the major difficulties in marriage, and that is violence. It is not unusual that I deal with couples who are regularly doing serious damage to each other. Broken bones, lacerations, black eyes, sprains and pulled muscles are nothing unusual. But when Paul said, "So ought men to love their wives as their own bodies" (Eph. 5:28), he was simply saying that you take care of your spouse exactly as you would take care of yourself. If you believe that beating your husband or your wife is the correct thing for you to do, then as an experiment you might put your hand on a table, pick up a hammer, and begin beating your own hand with the hammer that you hold in your other hand. I do not believe that any right-thinking individual would continue to beat it long, or would probably even make the first hit. This is what the apostle meant when he wrote that husbands and wives are part of each other, just as the organs are part of the body and complement each other.

Furthermore, if we take time for equality in the home it is difficult for us to separate so clearly, as some people do, the idea of man's work and woman's work. Wouldn't it be peculiar if the hand said to the feet, "I am not going to do that because that is your work"? Even when we are walking the hands help us keep balance. When we are picking things up the feet help us. They keep us upright. So the entire body works—here is that word again—together. Take time for equality. Work together as a family for a common goal and a common purpose.

Eternal Things

It certainly would not be fitting to close a book about marriage, the family, and the home without mentioning things of an eternal nature. The first time we read about the family is in the Bible, in the Book of Genesis. The family is the oldest institution known to man. God established the family for a purpose and this purpose still remains lofty—for the well-being of humanity.

As a family unit we should not forget our Creator. Therefore, we should take time for eternal things. If you consider the amount of time that we have on earth, you will recognize that if we live the allotted time to which the Lord makes reference, we will be able to spend ten years on Sundays. Every week has a first day and this day is referred to in the Bible as the Lord's day. Out of every 168 hours in every week there are 24 hours that belong to the Lord's day. So when we consider this, then we can hardly go many days without coming to a time when we need to think of eternal things.

Even society helps us think about eternal things. The vast majority of jobs are Monday through Friday or Saturday, with Sunday off. Even the newspaper is a bit different on Sunday. Stores that stay open on Sunday may have different hours. And on the Lord's day, churches that believe in Christ open their doors and welcome their constituents. All over the world there seems to be a quieting on the Lord's day. This is the one way that the family is reminded to think on eternal things. Take time to think on eternal things. You work the other days during the week, but on the Lord's day, spend time with your family to think on things eternal.

Heaven is such a grand and glorious place that the Bible describes it as a mansion that Jesus is preparing. He leaves the impression that heaven will be like a family situation. We are going to be members of that heavenly household.

To take time for things eternal means that we in our daily lives need to plan for Bible-study time and then on the Lord's day worship together as husband and wife.

I am well aware of the fact that worship without action is not of great value. But also I am aware of the fact that the more we attend the services, the more we listen. The more we pray and study, the more possiblility that His word will influence our lives. You are living in a divine institution, the family. It behooves you to study the Guide Book that tells us how to live in this God-ordained institution for which He has given rules and directions about how to conduct ourselves.

Taking time for eternal things means we will take our children to church with us. We will read Bible story books to them. We will study the Bible with them and teach them how to pray. When we sit down at meals we should pray and thank God for that which we have.

When we give children their allowances or get our wages for a week's work we will set aside a part for divine things.

Taking time for eternity means that we are conscious of the fact that there is an eternity and that we are preparing for it now.